After reading Russian at Merton College, Oxford, John C Q Roberts worked in Africa and Europe with Shell International for four years. He then spent a decade teaching foreign languages at Marlborough College. From there, in 1974, he was recruited to an official public post in Russo-British cultural relations. An account of his two decades as Director of the Great Britain-USSR Association and the Britain-Russia Centre was the subject of his book *Speak Clearly into the Chandelier*.

The author was awarded literary prizes in Russia following the appearance of his book there in translation.

For my children and grandchildren, thanking them for happy memories.

John C Q Roberts

# JUST BEFORE THE DAWN

## Tales of Late Colonial Africa

*For Hugh*
*with best wishes*
*John Robts*

AUSTIN MACAULEY PUBLISHERS™

LONDON • CAMBRIDGE • NEW YORK • SHARJAH

A CIP catalogue record for this title is available from the British Library.

ISBN 9781398485396 (Paperback)
ISBN 9781035810239 (Hardback)
ISBN 9781398485402 (ePub e-book)

www.austinmacauley.com

First Published 2022
Austin Macauley Publishers Ltd®
1 Canada Square
Canary Wharf
London
E14 5AA

# Table of Contents

# 1
# Getting There

It was 1957. Suitcases did not yet have fitted wheels. In the damp and dark of a February dawn a lone figure was hauling his luggage along a still empty London street.

After a fitful night in the station hotel, the young man was making his way towards premises on the Buckingham Palace Road. In those days the ground floor of the towering white building opposite Victoria Coach Station housed the point of departure for coaches delivering travellers fifteen miles along the old Bath Road to a group of Nissen huts which served as passenger terminal on the site of what would become the capital's busiest airport, Heathrow.

Nowadays I find it hard to credit that the person struggling with his luggage so long ago was truly none other than myself, setting out on a career in the international oil industry which could have continued through to retirement. In fact it lasted only four years, after which life was to take so many different turns that what went before seems like the experience of a complete stranger. I particularly regret that my time in Africa has faded, though traces of it remain in my mind and heart, as well as photos in old albums.

According to the French, l'appetit vient en mangeant.[1] Something similar may happen with these searches down my African memory lane. It could be simply nostalgia that prompts one in old age to recall significant times in life, or might it, in my case, have been the recently devoured volumes of Somerset Maugham's short stories from the Orient?

Let us return to that young man on the Buckingham Palace Road. On my last evening in England I remember feeling rotten after the yellow-fever and other jabs. I must have been poor company for my dear parents, who had come up from Cambridge for the day to take me to a matinee of *Under Milk Wood* at the New Theatre,[2] followed by a farewell dinner.

I may also have felt uneasy at the prospect of a long-haul flight. I had only been 'up' twice before, during National Service; first in an old Avro Anson from RAF Debden and then in an equally elderly Lancaster from RAF St Mawgan, both flights remembered as smelly, noisy and uncomfortable, though, thankfully, of short duration.

So for several reasons I might have felt something akin to the nervousness of a soldier on the eve of battle. There was another unhappy factor. I might never again see A. My first home-leave would be in three years. By then I would have lost her.

The flight did not live down to my expectations of it, but much the reverse. It has to be remembered that England was then rather a drab place. Everybody looked drab too. The end of clothes-rationing was still fresh in people's minds. Our

---

[1] Eating brings on the appetite.
[2] Now the Noël Coward Theatre

cities reeked of coal fires, as did our clothes. The Clean Air Act of 1956 had yet to affect the situation.

It had therefore been a surreal experience to go to the high-class men's outfitters, Messrs Airey and Wheeler of Savile Row, to acquire at my employer's expense what was deemed necessary for a gentleman's tropical wardrobe. The list included, for example, a dozen sea-island white cotton shirts, more shirts than I had ever possessed simultaneously. As the equivalent of a London business suit, for the East African coast 'sir' would also need to have white shorts and long white stockings, to be worn with shiny black shoes. For evening wear, he had to have a dinner suit, but with a white Tuxedo jacket, the latter a glamorous luxury, then only known to me from Hollywood films.

As for that very long flight to Kenya, here again one should reflect on the context. Air travel then catered for an elite. Holidays on Greek Islands or the Costas, the 'swinging sixties' and the rest were yet to come. Stepping out of the makeshift terminal into the BOAC Argonaut felt like a step into a new and privileged future.

The plane offered spacious and luxurious comfort together with superb service. Breakfast might well have included a glass of champagne, but I clearly remember the immaculate table-linen, the sparkling glasses and table-ware – also a feeling of disbelief. The next treat after breakfast was looking down on the Alps. With its four Rolls Royce Merlin piston engines, the Argonaut's cruising altitude was only about fifteen thousand feet, so the view was spectacular.

A further limitation was the operating range of the aircraft, meaning we had to make a refuelling stop at Rome, at its old Ciampino Airport, Leonardo da Vinci not yet having been constructed. The following 'hop' would have been to Cairo, but the Suez crisis the previous year had closed that route (along with Shell's business in Egypt), so we headed down Italy's west coast towards Libya. A memorable sight against the setting sun over the glistening sea was the perfect cone of the island of Stromboli, and the dark plume of its active volcano.

Dinner had been served and night fallen by the time we next landed, apparently in the middle of a desert. The only lights I remember were the flares in the sand, marking the landing strip. The crew announced that we had arrived at Benghazi, but I wonder whether it was some military base.

I have no recollection of leaving the aircraft there, so my first conscious step onto African soil was at our next refuelling stop. This was in the small hours at the Sudanese capital, Khartoum. Ah, the warmth of the African night! The chirping of the cicadas! And the waiters, all in ankle-length white linen, fez-topped, and padding silently barefoot over the stone floor of the softly lit transit lounge. The scene heightened the sense that I was entering upon a new life.

I was once amused by a cartoon showing a pupil desperate to catch teacher's attention. His arm achingly upstretched, he eventually cries, 'Please, sir, my brain is full.' Perhaps mine was too, since I have no recall of reaching Entebbe. By the time of that Ugandan stop we were into our second day in the air. Nor can I remember anything of the arrival and formalities at Nairobi Airport, nor of the transfer to the city-centre hotel, named after the explorer who, meeting another in the middle of African nowhere, had famously declared, 'Doctor Livingstone, I presume.'

# 2

# First Days in East Africa

The Norfolk, standing in its own gardens, was Nairobi's most elegant hotel, but the New Stanley, the largest, was situated in the commercial heart of the city on its principal street, Delamere Avenue,[3] as was Shell's East Africa Head Office.

After a quick freshening-up in my room, I went down to lunch. I remember a large, bright, high-ceilinged space, crowded with people all looking very fit, prosperous and relaxed. Although the worst Mau Mau troubles had died down, it was reassuring to observe such normality. Were it not for the plentiful non-white faces, it could have been the usual Saturday morning luncheon crowd in the main hotel of an English cathedral city.

Not yet accustomed to the tropical temperature, I made straight for the sumptuous cold buffet display and grabbed a couple of slices of melon. The thought of chilled melon in February! With the first mouthful, I realised this was neither melon, nor anything I had ever eaten. Nor was the taste at all to my liking. A waiter explained that it was pawpaw. I have never learned to like it.

---

[3] Nowadays Kenyatta Avenue

I was told I would shortly be posted south to neighbouring Tanganyika,[4] the former German colony administered by the United Kingdom as a United Nations trust territory. My few days in Nairobi were spent at the Head Office, acclimatising, getting to know the structure of the company and the people it would be useful to have met. It was soon apparent that many of my new colleagues were locally engaged from amongst the European community, rather than sent in from the company's world headquarters, as I had been. This did give rise to an 'us and them' culture, which could cause tensions.

There was one significant individual, Nikodem Muriuki, a recent graduate of Makerere University. He was the first African to be appointed as a salaried executive by any of the major businesses in Nairobi. Bright and personable he was. It came as no surprise to see the fulsome obituary notices published following his death in 2019, aged 89. Nik Muriuki had ended his career in oil as chief executive of the Shell Company of Kenya. In active retirement he remained a much-respected public figure both in his own country and beyond.

The Dakota flight down to Dar es Salaam, the Tanganyikan capital, took one past Mount Kilimanjaro with Kibo, (fig.1) its main peak, looking rather like a gigantic plum pudding, snow and ice rather than custard, dripping down its flanks. It was an impressive sight, if less dramatic than the Alps seen from the BOAC Argonaut.[5] As can be seen, the

---

[4] Tanganyika had not yet merged with Zanzibar to become today's Tanzania.

[5] It is alarming to look at today's photos of Kilimanjaro and see how little 'white custard' remains visible from across the plains.

Dakota's cruising altitude of 17,500ft is lower than the height of the mountain.

1

Little did I know then, as I looked across at the nineteen-thousand-foot giant, that the Shell Co. of East Africa would later send me on a team-work and character-building course at the Outward Bound movement's school at Loitokitok, a remote village tucked under the mountain on the Kenyan north side.

The Dakota DC3 from which I saw Kilimanjaro that day was a plane that one had seen in the air hundreds of times during the war, an all-purpose work-horse. In an article published by Boeing, it was written up thus:

*This was the plane that changed the way the world flew. The DC-3 made commercial air travel popular and airlines profitable and possible. Its commercial and military service over seven decades has made it an aviation legend.*

This thirty-seater flew most of East African Airways' internal routes, so I would soon get used to it, to the slope of its cabin rising to the horizontal as the tail-wheel left the ground and the plane hopefully gathered enough speed to take to the air. There would be destinations where business had to be pursued that only had short grass landing-strips. To reach such remote places, inaccessible by road in the rainy season, I could hire a single-engined Cessna from a private hire company in Dar. One of my regular pilots was memorably named Bill Dove, a moustachioed wartime RAF veteran. I was also provided with a brand-new long wheelbase Land Rover.

I dwell on the subject of transport, if only to emphasise the cultural shock I was undergoing. Only weeks before, I had been a poorly dressed and unwaged youngster in damp, drab

England, whose only private means of travel was a slow, smelly and second-hand BSA Bantam two-wheeler.

Perhaps I sported my new Tuxedo on one of my first evenings in the Tanganyikan capital where night falls at about six o'clock. I found myself under the stars on the terrace of Dar's New Africa Hotel overlooking the harbour, apparently the smartest place for sundowners. The people seemed subtly different from the Nairobi crowd, certainly more mixed, less English. Tanganyika had never had such a dominant settler presence as had Kenya. The majority at such watering-holes might be smartly dressed professionals (lawyers or engineers, for example), or independent businessmen.

Suddenly I noticed a familiar neck-tie, dark blue with slanting yellow stripes, that of University College Oxford. Then to my astonishment I realised that it was around the neck of a young Indian who was a student friend and contemporary. I had known he came from somewhere in Africa, but either had forgotten or had never bothered to memorise the details. Sukhi Singh's father had recently died, so he was home helping his mother keep their ships' chandler business afloat. He later embarked on an international career with the Asian Development Bank, based in the Philippines.

He introduced me on that first evening, and later, to some of his friends, mostly Asians or Zanzibaris. It was a good way of getting a feel for the place and for developing contacts. Before long, one of these, an Asian lawyer, invited Sukhi and me to dinner at his home, saying his English wife was always glad to meet someone freshly arrived from London.

The only other dinner guest was a client of his, an up and coming African, a graduate of Edinburgh University. He was very knowledgeable and happy to discuss current political developments in Britain with us two youngsters, both ten years his junior, and to share his hopes for the future of his own country. Only four years later, he would become Prime Minister Julius Nyerere and, shortly thereafter, the first President of an independent Tanganyika.

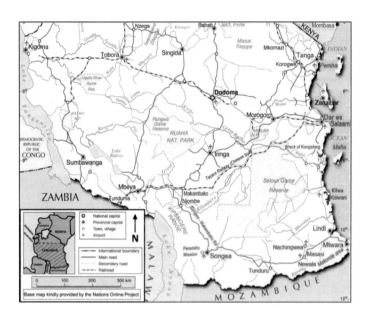

Plate 1: Map of Tanzania Southern Province and related areas up
the East coast.

# 3

# Tanganyika

Shell's offices in Dar es Salaam were adjacent to the docks and the petroleum storage facilities. The surroundings had a much more industrial feel than did the company HQ in Nairobi's tree-lined Delaware Avenue. A pervasive smell of oil hung in the air, accentuated by the high coastal humidity. One appreciated the cool clean air of the air-conditioned offices – and the shirt and shorts dress-code. (fig.2 *The staff of Shell Co. of Tanganyika, the author third from left back row*). Few comforts would probably await me in the Southern Province which I was about to take over. It was reputed in several ways to be a difficult posting. A day or so before taking it up, I was summoned to our managing director's office.[6] I anticipated this might be for an encouraging chat.

---

[6] He was of South African origin and would shortly be replaced.

2

The conversation quickly took an unpleasant turn. He had heard that I had been 'associating with the natives' and this had to stop, or he would send me back to London. I countered by telling him that in London our intake of arts graduates, recruited to bring fresh blood into the management of Shell's world-wide empire, had been expressly instructed during our training to get to know 'coming people' in the countries to which we would be assigned. I thought that I had already done rather well in that respect and said so, adding that I would report our conversation back to London. This was in 1957, three years before Harold Macmillan's 'Winds of Change' speech in Cape Town.

There the matter rested. My knees not yet brown, I took up responsibility for the Southern Province. With an area about the size of Wales, its commercial significance was then perhaps equivalent to that of little Anglesey. The area had a large African population, mostly subsistence farmers with little mechanisation. Such trade as went on was almost entirely in the hands of Asians of Indian origin. Much of my business would be with them.

The Southern Province had been chosen for the British post-war government's ill-conceived Groundnut Scheme. The area in question was some two hundred kilometres inland from the especially developed deep-water port of Mtwara. Apart from the few expatriate farmers who had stayed on up-country struggling to establish private farms after the costly failure of that Scheme, there might only have been a few dozen Europeans in the whole Southern Province. A 'rough diamond' from Yorkshire ran Mtwara's only hotel. I heard years later that he was expelled from the country for calling his dog 'Julius'.

I remember as well, and with profound respect, many extraordinary fellow-Europeans: the missionaries, district officers, the telephone engineer, a judge, a doctor and others. Often working in tough and lonely places, such people's dedication to the material and spiritual progress of others should come to mind when one is confronted with the infantile posturing fashionable today in the 'mother country' and, alas, in its universities.

I set off by Dakota from Dar with Michael Clayton,[7] whom I was replacing. Flying south parallel to the coast, the route soon took us across the Rufiji Delta. The remains of the

---

[7] Mike and I have since remained in contact. He eventually left Shell, emigrating to Australia, where I once had the pleasure of seeing him again.

German light battlecruiser, *SMS Königsberg,* were still visible lying on her side in the mangrove swamp where she had sought to hide. In 1914 and 1915 the warship had been at the centre of a prolonged and important battle in the Great War. Perhaps here was an historic first in air-sea co-ordination. Observer aircraft, flying from nearby Mafia Island, had guided the guns of the British destroyers pursuing the ship from outside the delta.

Some of the German crew escaped and joined the forces led by General Paul von Lettow-Vorbeck. Known to history as the 'Lion of Africa', he and those under his command, fought on until surrendering in November 1918 in what was Northern Rhodesia, today's Zambia. Not all of his men had survived. By the road-side one would come across an occasional simply fenced German burial-ground. For some reason I picture one in particular, close to the Anglican mission near Lindi at Masasi, where Trevor Huddleston, the well-known anti-apartheid campaigner, was soon to be installed as bishop.

Back to the handover safari,[8] we first dropped off some passengers at Lindi, then flew the short leg further south to disembark at Mtwara. The town lies a few miles north of the mouth of the Rovuma River (then yet to be bridged), which formed the frontier between Tanganyika and the then Portuguese colony of Mozambique, nowadays an independent member of the Commonwealth.

Due to the Groundnut Scheme, Mtwara, basically a new town, had a grandiose urban plan. Apart from the deep-water port, nothing much had been actually realised there. Only one

---

[8] A Swahili word derived from the Arabic for travel.

lane of the dual carriageway of its projected main street had been laid and there were no buildings on it apart from the Shell petrol station. The latter had a ludicrously long approach road, because it was not even built on the lane that did exist, but beyond the planned second lane on a separate side-plot.

One of our inland destinations during the handover was the township of Nachingwea, developed as the terminus for a railway that used to link it to Mtwara, from where the groundnut crop was to be exported. There had also been an oil pipeline leading from the new port up to bulk storage facilities at Nachingwea. The pipeline had already been dismantled and reportedly sold to the Israeli government. The level in the remaining isolated storage tank was getting low. Customers were finding water in their fuel. To such problems, I had to find solutions.

In Nachingwea we stayed in the simple yet clean government guesthouse. At our next destination, the long-established coastal town of Lindi, we stayed in the only hotel, sometimes referred to as the 'Dysentery Arms'.(fig.3 *'Dysentery Arms', beach)* On the main street into the town, it occupied a beautiful position on a sandy beach looking across an estuary to hills covered with sisal plantations. (figs.4 and 5) I would often stay in Lindi because our most important Asian dealership was there.

3

4

5

The hotel is probably now a modernised holiday hide-out with air-conditioning, but I remember the flies, the unspeakable toilets, the torn mosquito-nets, but the absolutely delicious fish. My fondness for the place was reflected in my giving the name Lindi to the first house we bought after my eventual return to live in England. There was another reason: in its main street I first noticed the good-looking girl I later married. I also remember a flying (literally) visit I once made to Lindi, Bill Dove in his Cessna landing me and a visiting VIP on the curved sandy beach, having first made a low-level pass to frighten off the fishermen.(fig.6)

6

Most of my travelling, however, was by Land Rover. None of the roads in the Southern Province were macadamed in those days. In dry weather you could see the distant dust-cloud trailing behind an oncoming vehicle. Despite the stifling heat in the cabin, it was vital to close the front vents before plunging blind into that cloud. On the other hand, in wet weather the problem was to keep the vehicle on the slippery murram roadway.

Another hazard was the wild-life, although where I went, there was little in terms of 'big game'. Often driving in the dark, through the clouds of night insects, I learned to recognise serval cats, and other nocturnal creatures, briefly caught in the headlights. By day I sometimes saw troops of baboon who could be aggressive, or the shy and beautiful colobus monkeys always quietly browsing up in the trees.

Once I was driving fast along a straight stretch, the low early sun casting sharply defined shadows onto the road, whether of trees such as the stout baobabs, or of pyramidic ant-heaps. I remember driving towards and over one thin straight 'shadow' and being surprised to feel a double jolt from my front and rear wheels. Instinctively glancing in my rear view mirror, I saw an enormous snake flailing in the dust cloud, with its pale underside visible. I stopped and reversed warily to the spot but found nothing, so the creature, probably a python, must have survived. And the thin dark line across the roadway was no more.

One of my favourite calling places was Newala, some seventy-five miles inland from Mtwara. The village was perched on the lip of the escarpment of the Makonde plateau above the Rovuma River and enjoyed a panoramic view, dotted with strange *Inselberge,* remnants of the cores of long extinct volcanoes. (fig.7) Southwards, it looked down over the forest towards the wide, but shallow river, and far beyond it, into Mozambique. For the hell of it, I once persuaded a local fisherman to pole me across the Rovuma in his dug-out, risking crocodiles and illegally entering remote Portuguese territory.(figs.8 and 9) I gave him an apple, for him an exotic fruit. He mimed that he would plant the pips.

7

8

9

10

Over a hundred and fifty years ago David Livingstone's second expedition to the Zambezi passed this way (fig.10) and recorded the strange Rovuma River landscape. The engraving was published in London by John Murray in 1865.(fig.11)

Due to the proximity of water, the Makonde population had concentrated over time along the escarpment edge. The result was that the land there was overworked, with overpopulation leading to poverty and disease. The colonial government decided to invest in a pumping system. The Makonde Water Corporation was established, tasked with distributing water from the valley to the less populated fertile areas further into the plateau. The scheme would also liberate people, mostly women, from the unending task of bringing water up onto the plateau, in large urns balanced on their heads. (fig.10)

11

An English colonial servant, George Mitchell, was put in charge of the new corporation, which built a comfortable bungalow for him and for his hospitable family on the edge of the escarpment. Much of the pleasure of my visits to the Mitchells would have been that of a somewhat lonesome bachelor finding himself a guest in homely surroundings. As for business, I remember we discussed my proposal of setting up for kerosene sales at all the water distribution points. Four-gallon tins of the product, used for cooking and lighting, were a significant element in my turnover.

The Makonde tribe are famed wood-carvers, principally of ebony. Their works have become sought after by museums and collectors. I still possess some items bought in Newala from one old carver. Among them is a walking stick which has a snake spiralling up it with an inlaid silvery dorsal streak, probably fashioned from a melted-down aluminium saucepan. It is seen in the cover picture of the author.

I asked him to make me an all-ebony paper-knife with the handle end in the form of a scallop shell. I sent the resulting sample to our Nairobi office, suggesting it could replace in East Africa some of the cheap and nasty shell-embossed plastic hand-outs that were on offer world-wide for publicity and good-will purposes. That idea was not pursued. More than sixty years later I have it on my desk and use it daily, an elegant Makonde souvenir. (fig.12)

12

My territory stretched some four hundred miles inland westwards from Mtwara and Lindi on the coast up to the eastern shore of Lake Nyasa, nowadays called Lake Malawi.

The furthest I ever penetrated was to Songea, about a hundred miles short of the lake, and home to one of the largest RC missions in Africa, Peramiho.[9]

On one occasion, when I needed to get there, my Land Rover broke down just as I was leaving Newala on the long and lonely road, which was little more than a rough track in the sand. The only solution was for me to hire from our Newala dealer his pick-up truck and driver. I remember the sign at the counter in his *duka:* 'In God we trust. Others pay cash.'

Half-way to Songea, the driver lost control. Perhaps he had fallen asleep. We left the road, smashing through the undergrowth and trees until hitting one thick enough to bring us to a halt. My knees crashed into the dashboard, there being no fitted seatbelts in those days. It was an hour or two before another vehicle came along. Fortunately, it was my telephone engineer friend, heading back towards the coast, and to medical assistance.

One thing that made life in this 'poor relation' province somewhat more manageable was the British India Line's little M/V Mombasa which plied up and down the coast, delivering fresh produce from Kenya such as meat, fruit and vegetables. It also had a small number of passenger cabins. Thus, up-country Kenyans could spend a pleasant fortnight at sea level, cruising from Mombasa, calling at Tanga, Zanzibar, Dar,

---

[9] Peramiho was later visited by HRH the Princess Anne at the suggestion of my cousin, Jonathan Roberts, the construction engineer on a major road project that she had come to open.

Kilwa, Lindi and Mtwara before heading back north to Mombasa.

Kilwa, then hardly known to the outside world, is a very special place. It has existed since the eighth century. Its island, Kilwa Kisiwani, has recently been declared a UNESCO World Heritage Site. In the Middle Ages this small hamlet, nowadays with a thousand or so inhabitants, had a population of ten thousand. For five hundred years, until about 1600, Kilwa minted its own coins. A visitor from Morocco in 1331 had called it one of the most beautiful cities in the world. All I was to see were remote crumbling ruins with little sign of any attempt to preserve them.[10]

I was somewhere up-country when a message from Head Office reached me. I had to get to Kilwa to sort out a problem. It was the rainy season. One of our underground petrol storage tanks had started lifting, so the matter was urgent. The roads along the coast were impassable. Fortunately, I knew that the M/V Mombasa was about to head north back from Mtwara to Lindi and would then call at Kilwa, so I hurried down to the coast.

As I drove into Lindi, the presence on the street of European strangers confirmed that the ship had arrived. (In such places European pedestrians were a rare sight.) Near the 'Dysentery Arms' I saw a middle-aged couple accompanied by the aforementioned attractive girl, presumably their daughter. They would be my overnight travelling companions to Kilwa and onwards to Dar. The family was from Nairobi and would become very much part of my life when I

---

[10] The full story can be found on Wikipedia. Likewise information on 'The battle of the Rufiji Delta'.

subsequently left Tanganyika for Kenya. The daughter and I spent a pleasant hour or so collecting coloured glass beads on a sandy beach below Kilwa's ruins, evidence of its early connections to Persia and Ceylon.(fig.13)

13

At some point during my stint in the Southern Province there was a *baraza,* this being the Swahili word for a tribal council gathering. This one must have been called by the authorities because it was attended not only by the provincial commissioner and all his district officers, but by the Governor of Tanganyika himself, Sir Edward Twining (of the tea family), who had had a distinguished colonial service career and an important but, for some years afterwards, secret war record. It must have been part of his farewell safari before he retired in 1958 and joined the Upper House as The Rt Hon Lord Twining of Tanganyika GCMG MBE KStJ.

It was a bright sunny day at the PC's *boma*.[11]

There we all were, with the tribal leaders in their best finery. The Governor, the PC and all his DOs wore the white dress uniform of the colonial service with white pith solar helmets, plumed in the Governor's case with ostrich feathers fluttering in the breeze.(fig.14) George Mitchell of the Makonde Water Corporation sported his well-deserved MBE. (fig.15)Together they made an arresting spectacle. (Were they all 'wicked colonialists'?) However, looking back at that scene, I admit to thinking of the over-the-top finale of a musical or a pantomime. Removing my clothes that night, I was mortified to find that I had spent the day with unbuttoned flies. Back then, like suit-cases with wheels, fly-zips on men's trousers were not yet common currency.

14

---

[11] Originally an animal stockade, later extended to mean a guarded outstation.

15

To finish with the Southern Province, much of it included the Selous Game Reserve, the largest in Africa, and possibly the least accessible of them. It had been established in 1922. For me to penetrate so far into the empty *bundu*[12] would have been unjustifiable, and perhaps risky to attempt alone. It teemed with game of every kind. Unlike now, there was no organised tourism, and even today no permanent human habitation is allowed in the Selous Reserve, with every exit and entry requiring a government permit.

The Selous Reserve was the hunting ground of the celebrated snake-collector, C J P Ionides. Known locally as 'Iodine', he lived in Newala. Regrettably, he and I somehow never met. He died in 1968 in Nairobi but lies buried inside the Reserve along with the British explorer and naturalist in whose memory the reserve is named.

---

[12] Uninhabited wilderness, a Swahili word derived from Shona.

Frederick C Selous (1851–1917), a friend of Cecil Rhodes and Theodore Roosevelt, died in action against General von Lettow-Vorbeck's Deutsch-Ostafrika forces in the Rufiji Delta. A few weeks later his son was killed in action over Belgium. Like his comrades in the Royal Naval Air Service on far away Mafia Island, the young man was a military pilot.

Now let us fly to Zanzibar!

# 4

# Zanzibar

Imagine Kilwa Kisiwani as it would have been in its heyday, centuries ago. That is what met my eye on first seeing Zanzibar – its harbour and town bustling with life and energy, the comings and goings of Arab sailing dhows from the Gulf, of local fishing boats and the big ships of the Union Castle Line and the British-India Steamship Navigation Company. (fig.16)

16

Nowadays, Zanzibar is part of an independent Tanzania, but then it was a separate protectorate managed by a British Resident under an elderly ruling Sultan, the last but two of the line established in 1856. Khalifa bin Haroub was said to have been to London for the celebration of Queen Victoria's Diamond Jubilee. He subsequently ruled for nearly fifty years until his death in October 1960.

The island and its dependencies, lying in the Indian Ocean some seventy-five kilometres off Dar es Salaam, had a long and complex history, even before they were ceded by Germany to the United Kingdom in 1890 in exchange for Heligoland. Shortly afterwards the Sultan of the day had signed the edict abolishing slavery in the sultanate, which earned him a knighthood. Zanzibar's Anglican cathedral now stands on the site of East Africa's last slave market.

One element, apart from the slave trade, had long played an important part in the Zanzibar economy. Its neighbouring dependent island of Pemba is one of the world's major producers of cloves and other spices. Before export, the crop is brought to dockside warehouses in Zanzibar's ancient Stone Town, the aroma of spice all-pervading.

I suppose it was Shell's idea that whoever carried the little coveted responsibility for its business in the tough and rough Southern Province of Tanganyika should be compensated with the pleasure of managing the company's affairs in this exotic outpost. The only way for me to get to Zanzibar was by ship or plane from Dar. Thus I was not condemned to live permanently in places like Lindi's beautifully situated, yet squalid hotel, even if the fish had been good.

According to the brochures, there are now plentiful modern hotels dotted around Zanzibar's multitude of perfect beaches. Then there was only one place where a tourist or businessman could stay, the Zanzibar Hotel. Run by an English couple, it was an old building in the Stone Town near the Sultan's Palace. In its cosy little bar one would meet habitués from every milieu, the clientele even more mixed than in Dar. There was, to mention but a few, a Comoran playboy, an exiled East European princess with her African partner, the Asian Chief of Police, the British captain of the Sultan's yacht and, of course, hotel residents such as myself. The Sultan's eldest grandson, Prince Jamshid, a dashing young man of about my age, owner of a bright-red sports car, could also be encountered there.

Many years later he would become the last Sultan of Zanzibar, overthrown only a few weeks into his reign by a bloody revolution. At ninety-one years of age he returned to Oman, the land of his ancestors. Before that he had lived for over fifty years quietly in exile in Southsea. A less quiet future lay ahead of another refugee from that revolution – the Zanzibar-born lead vocalist of Queen, Freddy Mercury.

On one particular evening in the hotel bar I was chatting with an East African Airways pilot. It turned out that he would be doing the scheduled flight to Pemba and back the following day. I was booked on that service myself. Captain Robinson remarked that he would be sailing between Zanzibar and Pemba at the time of our return flight in the afternoon. I had just bought a good camera and suggested some aerial photography.

The following morning, we flew the eighty kilometres to Pemba, its airport terminal being a small mud-hut roofed with palm fronds. (fig.17) We were in a de Havilland Rapide biplane which had some eight seats.[13] For the afternoon flight back to Zanzibar, I was installed in the front seat behind the pilot, able to see over his shoulder. Shortly after take-off, he spotted the H.H.S. Seyyid Khalifa a long way below us and put the plane into a dive. Soon we were flying just above sea level. There had been no passenger announcement. I imagined the other passengers behind me, local Muslims, silently praying while we whizzed round and round the Sultan's yacht, with Captain Robinson up on his bridge waving as I snapped.(fig.18) On behalf of Shell I sent one of the photos to the Sultan and received a letter conveying thanks from His Highness. (fig.19 *Coming in to land at Zanzibar)*

17

---

[13] Curiously, the family running the Zanzibar Hotel also bore the name of de Havilland.

18

19

I was dismayed to hear news of the revolution and accompanying heavy loss of life in 1964.[14] Zanzibar had struck me as rather stable and peaceful. Maybe trouble-fomenters from elsewhere, such as Egypt's Gamal Nasser who had overthrown the monarchy there and expropriated the Suez Canal, had been waiting for the revolutionary opportunity that would present itself in Zanzibar under a new and untried Sultan, a chance to end two centuries of Arab dominance over the native Zanzibaris.

I took my new camera once to a football match. It might have been an important fixture. The modest stadium was packed and the almost-80-year-old Sultan came with his son and grandsons.(figs.20 and 21) He was cheered by the crowd as he arrived. One of my photographs shows him smiling and waving. At the match he had no armed escorts.

20

---

[14] By then I was permanently back in England.

21

Similarly, on his regular late afternoon drive, His Highness would be accompanied only by his chauffeur. At about half past five on most days, the bright-red Armstrong Siddeley would be seen quietly emerging through the gates of the palace (fig.22) to proceed smoothly along past the rickshaw stand and the waterfront gardens, where people would be enjoying the cooler clove-scented air. Individuals would wave and the elderly Sultan would wave in reply from the back of the car.

22

Then, to the sound of distant music coming from the Victorian bandstand beside the British Resident's fine galleried house overlooking the sea, and with the sun's orange ball sinking into a misted horizon, the red limousine would turn the corner and be gone. (fig.23)

23

A final nocturnal moment from one of Zanzibar's deserted beaches comes to mind, a surreal memory. Perhaps it was the full moon that prompted the crabs to emerge in multitude from the sand higher up the beach in order to go down to the water. The sport was to chase back and forth between the advancing hordes and the water's edge so as to frighten the crabs back towards their holes. In the end, they always won.

It is now time to say '*Kwa heri,* Zanzibar!' with all its charm, and '*Jambo,* Kenya!'

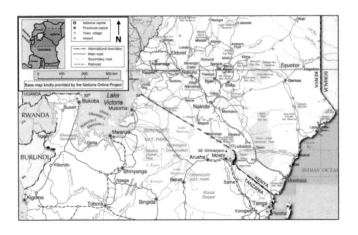

Plate 2: Map of Kenya, and related areas in northern Tanzania,
also showing the locations of Rwanda and Burundi.
© Copyright: One World – Nations Online, OWNO,
nationsonline.org. Editor Klaus Kästle. All rights reserved.

# 5

# Kenya

The Swahili for *goodbye, hallo* and many other everyday words will be found deeply embedded in the memory of anybody who has spent a while in East Africa. The country itself exerts a continuing hold on one. Clearly it has in my case. Perhaps it is the beauty and variety of the endless landscapes, or the wild-life, combined with the unspoilt charm of its indigenous inhabitants.

Leaving such thoughts to one side, I admit I had begun, at the time, to miss the cultural riches (theatres, concerts, art exhibitions) that had been part of my daily environment in Oxford, Cambridge or London. Life in Tanganyika and Zanzibar had offered little or none of that.

There was, however, one shop in Dar which sold classical and other records. In the heat and humidity of the Indian Ocean coast it was refreshing to listen to Peter Pears's interpretations of English folk-songs in the cool-sounding arrangements by Benjamin Britten, with the composer accompanying Pears on piano. I still have that vinyl. Another one included a helpfully 'coolant' track: Ella Fitzgerald and Louis Armstrong in haunting duet with *A Foggy Day in London Town.*

In that sense my transfer from the heat and humidity of the coast to upland Kenya came as a relief. In addition, there would be a sophisticated side to life – parties, theatre, dances, concerts. The move also offered the pleasant prospect of seeing D again from time to time, the girl with whom I had gathered ancient beads in the sand at Kilwa. Her parents lived in a bungalow in the grounds of Nairobi's All Saints Cathedral. She worked as a secretary in a government office. As pets, they had a monkey and a sealyham terrier.

Her father, a retired major, had been wounded in the battle for Sicily. Later, I believe, he was seconded to the King's African Rifles. By the time I knew him, he was working in the Kenya Government's Mau Mau prison camps. His function was to decide which detainees could or should be released for rehabilitation. One of these had become his long-serving and much loved and trusted houseboy. Their good relationship was reflected in that the servant named his many children after members of the family of his master – and saviour. The major was an exceptionally kind-hearted man, later to become an adored grandfather to my children.

My new posting meant living some 160 kilometres further up-country from Nairobi at Nakuru, a town in the Rift Valley about half-way between the capital and Lake Victoria, and central to the White Highlands. This was the area with the greater part, as now, of the country's agricultural production, including tea, coffee, sisal and pyrethrum.

I was responsible for the management and development of Shell's network of service stations in the White Highlands, requiring me to negotiate such things as property deals and planning applications. Not particularly interesting work, but it enabled me to drive in the company's comfortable saloon virtually anywhere over the most beautiful country imaginable, one with a delightful climate. Little wonder the area was chosen for European settlement at the turn of the twentieth century.

Social life centred on the local country clubs that the settlers established, usually in splendid locations. I used to enjoy staying in them. The Soy Club near Eldoret, with its little quadrangle of bungalows surrounding a beautifully tended and very English garden, was one place chosen for Princess Elizabeth's stay in Kenya with the Duke of Edinburgh, before they moved on to Treetops, and she to queenship.(fig.24)

24

Not far away was the Molo Club, its golf course boasting the highest tee in the British Empire, at over two and a half thousand metres above sea-level. I also recall a hilarious evening of amateur pantomime at the Nakuru Club, and a boring afternoon having to watch cars going round and round the town's motor-racing circuit.[15]

There were reports that some of those country clubs had difficulties in adapting after Kenya became independent, but it is good that many have survived the changes. Except for its ludicrously grand railway station, recently refurbished, the modest Nakuru that I knew with its avenues of jacaranda trees would now be unrecognisable to me. (figs.25 and 26)What the town cannot lose, however, is its famous lake, home to one of the country's natural wonders, a major tourist attraction.

25

---

[15] Since the 1980s a housing estate.

26

Only five minutes' drive from my bungalow, I used often to go down to the lakeside towards the end of the day to gaze at the millions of pink flamingos wading a few yards away in the shallow alkaline waters, foraging for algae and tiny crustaceans. (figs.27 and 28)There were always some in low flight, giving flashes of their other colours – black, white and ink-red. Usually I was the only human around. As a dubious bonus, the lane down to Lake Nakuru passed right beside the town's rubbish dump, frequented by its ugly congregation of enormous vultures.(fig.29)

27

28

29

There really were 'millions' of flamingos. Menengai, a volcano a couple of miles to the north, has one of the biggest craters in the world (12 by 8 km), itself a spectacular place. There was a track up it and from the crater rim one could look down on the whole lake five hundred metres below.(fig.30) At distance, it seemed as if there were wide beaches of pink sand around its shore.[16] On a clear day one could also see, like a cloud low on the horizon, the unmistakable white smudge of Kilimanjaro where Shell sent me to take a short 'holiday' at the Loitokitok Outward Bound School.

---

[16] Due to climate change and the loss of shallows, the flamingos abandoned this lake for a while, but are now returning, vital for Kenya's tourist industry.

30

Something unusual for its time about that challenging leaders' course was that young men sent on it came from all races. They were divided into teams of about eight, with a daily rotating leadership. In my boarding school there had been Ethiopians, Indians and others. In Kenya, apart from the physical proximity, the acceptance of being led sometimes by a non-European was a challenge for those who had only known such people as houseboys, clerks or shopkeepers. The non-Europeans in their turn would not have found it easy to find themselves in charge of individuals they may only have known as their 'superiors'.

The first day or two of the course was spent on fitness training and on cutting a path through the new growth of the thick forest that covers the lower slopes of the mountain. Then we had to push further up above the tree line to establish food and water depots for the final three-day assault on the summit, there being no natural springs higher up the mountain. We had neither guides nor porters, so those preliminary forays gave us some experience of the physical and mental effects of altitude.

To reach the summit the plan was to get to the Kibo Hut before nightfall on the second day of the climb. This simple hut was at the western end of the extensive saddle that stretches between Kibo and Kilimanjaro's rocky eastern peak, Mawenzi.(fig.31) At the hut it was a matter of trying to get some sleep until waking up at about three o'clock in the morning for the final stage of the climb.

31

The Kibo Hut (fig.32) was at the foot of the steep slope of the 'plum pudding'. The greater part of this last leg consisted of volcanic powdery scree which was only possible to deal with while it remained frosted. It would still be night when one reached the beginning of the ice. From then on, gasping for air, it was a question of groping in the dark and pulling oneself up step by step with the aid of one's ice-pick.

32

A memorable moment came when, stopping for a breather, one looked back eastwards onto the sixteen-thousand-foot Mawenzi at the other end of the saddle, some fifteen kilometres away. Having previously towered above us, Kilimanjaro's rocky eastern peak was now satisfyingly below our level, with the sun rising behind its rocky mass, illuminating the dawn clouds and the two lakes reflecting the sky.(fig.33)

33

With the sun up, there was no further need to keep together, so it was every man for himself to make it to Gilman's Point on the crater rim.(fig.34) Anticipating a possible photo, for the final ascent I had pulled on over my trousers a pair of red pyjama bottoms. I was new to colour photography, and a friend had told me how effective a splash of that colour could be. My appearance was a source of some merriment for the others. In those days gentlemen's trousers were only available in shades of grey or brown.(fig.35)

34

35

The fitter amongst us first to reach the crater rim had time to continue round to its very highest point, *Kaiser-Wilhelm-Spitze,* as it had been known since first being climbed during the German colonial period.[17] (fig.36) The descent was altogether a different matter. The pick was useful on the slippery ice, and when it came to the now unfrosted scree, one could slide down in a sitting position, some of us riskily using the pick as a sort of mono-ski held between the thighs.

36

Back at base, tired but uplifted by a sense of shared achievement, there was no chance to relax as there was to be a VIP inspection.(fig.37) On almost our last day at Loitokitok we were visited by no less than the Chief of the Imperial General Staff, the professional head of the British Army.(fig.38)

---

[17]Renamed Uhuru Peak since independence, it had been just inside Kenya until Queen Victoria reportedly gifted it to her nephew, the German Kaiser.

37

38

Field Marshall Sir Gerald Templer KG GCB KBE DSO,
who had fought in both world wars, had been the chief

military adviser to Prime Minister Eden during the recent Suez crisis. We were given to understand that Templer was making a stopover in East Africa during a flight back to London from Malaya.[18] The Outward Bound School was run on military lines under the command of a retired serving officer. For Templer the movement's fundamental purpose had obvious relevance to army training.

He spent some time discussing a diagram I had drawn with coloured chalks on a blackboard. It depicted our operation in all its stages. (figs.39 and 40)What we had achieved from the wilder north side of the mountain had nothing in common with the highly organised and guided routes that package tourists can attempt nowadays in their thousands from the south or east, having arrived comfortably at the nearby modern Kilimanjaro International Airport.

39

---

[18] Templer is remembered for his handling of the Malayan Emergency and his strategy for defeating the communist MNLA.

40

It was a pleasure to share some of my favourite places with my mother and father when they came from the English winter to stay with me at Nakuru late in 1958. They had their fill of them, the grandeur of the Rift Valley, the flamingos in their multitude, walking with baby elephant and rhino on the Carr-Hartleys' game farm at nearby Rumuruti. New generations of that family have since built up a successful safari business, as well as continuing to work in wild-life preservation. (fig.41)

41

It was a problem to persuade newly arrived visitors from home to walk wherever possible in the shade. I remember my '*Mad Dogs and Englishmen*'[19] parents enjoying the sun hatless at the point of maximum ultra-violet exposure where the road from Nakuru to Eldoret crossed the Equator at an altitude of 9109 feet. (fig.42)

---

[19] An expression said to have been originated by Rudyard Kipling, popularized by Noël Coward's 1931 song, *Mad dogs and Englishmen go out in the midday sun.*

42

To thank his parents for coming to Kenya for his wedding, their now comfortably independent son was happy to offer them and to his parents-in-law the same Treetops experience that their royal highnesses had enjoyed. I also treated them to a few nights on Zanzibar after the ceremony.

D and I were married in Nairobi's All Saints Cathedral on 10 January 1959 with Mike Clayton, then still with the Shell Company of East Africa, as my best man. We honeymooned in a country then called Ruanda-Urundi. That separate African story merits a brief chapter of its own.

# 6

# Ruanda-Urundi

On a cycling tour in my teens a schoolfriend and I passed through Rouen, still showing many signs of wartime destruction, not least at the ancient Abbey Church of St Ouen. That abbey is lucky to have what the French composer Charles-Marie Widor rated to be 'the Michelangelo of organs'. On the morning I was there, an organist happened to be practising Widor's Toccata. That first hearing had left an indelible impression on me. I suggested it for the end of our wedding service but was overruled. It was 'unknown' and *ipso facto* 'too modern' for our two rather conventional families.[20](fig.43)

---

[20] The Toccata from the 5th Organ Symphony has since become popular as a wedding march. It was chosen by the Duke and Duchess of Cambridge for their wedding at Westminster Abbey.

43

So our happy day followed the usual local conventions: Mike and I in morning dress, bridesmaids, a choir and Mendelssohn's March, followed by a reception at the Norfolk and a night at the Brown Trout, a rural weekend trysting place, conveniently close to Nairobi.[21] For going away, D wore a 'sack dress', the latest fashion from Paris.

If denied the unconventional in the music, I chose not to do the conventional thing, namely, not to honeymoon somewhere down on the Kenyan coast. I had long been intrigued by accounts of the Mountains of the Moon, the Ruwenzori and, beyond them, the mountains and lakes

---

[21] It closed in the '60s and is now a school.

sometimes referred to as the 'Switzerland of Africa', right in the middle of the continent. The states of Burundi and Rwanda, as they are now called, would be described by a British Ambassador in his initial despatch from there in 1964 as 'scenically two of the most beautiful countries I have ever visited'.[22]

Yet nobody I knew in East Africa ever spoke of venturing westwards to holiday in non-British colonial lands. It is ironic and tragic that, some years later, this magnificent area would witness mass murder in Africa's bloodiest tribal conflict, now remembered as the Rwandan Genocide.

One day in mid-January 1959 D and I took the Sabena flight from Nairobi to Bukavu in the Belgian Congo (today's Democratic Republic of the Congo). That town lies at the southwest corner of Lake Kivu. From there we took another flight with the same (later defunct) Belgian airline to Goma, still in the Belgian Congo, but some two hundred kilometres away at the northern end of the lake. It was during one of our flights that day that the pilot relayed to his passengers sensational news from Brussels: the Belgians were going to quit Africa, soon and suddenly.

Belgium already had an horrific back-story in Africa. To quote Matthew Parris and Andrew Bryson once more, 'In the 1870s ... King Leopold II seized the Congo, an area seventy-six times the size of Belgium, as his personal domain. Millions of Congolese died in the decades that followed through forced labour, shootings and disease.' Leopold was the founder and sole owner of what would become

---

[22] From *In The Spanish Ambassador's Suitcase* Ed. Matthew Parris and Andrew Bryson (Viking, 2012)

internationally recognised as the Congo Free State. To quote Wikipedia: 'In 1908, the reports of deaths and abuse and pressure from the Congo Reform Association and other international groups induced the Belgian government to take over the administration of the Congo from Leopold as a new territory, Belgian Congo.'

The years of colonial rule that followed may have seen an end to the atrocities, but the continuing story was primarily one of economic exploitation, with little or no push to improve the lives of the Congolese or to involve them in their country's administration, as had long been happening in British Africa, both East and West. The Belgians washed their hands of their totally unprepared colony in 1960, just a year after the surprise announcement we had heard in the aeroplane. Kenya and Tanganyika only gained their independence four years later, and each of them would enjoy a much surer start in life.

Though conscious of the implications of the Belgian decision, we happy honeymooners were over the moon about our choice of destination. The flight along Lake Kivu from Bukavu to Goma had given us a hint of the beautiful scenery that would be a source of wonder for a British Ambassador. From Goma it was only a few minutes' taxi ride along the tree-lined lake to the Ruanda-Urundi border and the lakeside hotel at Gisenyi, where the bedrooms were all simple rondavels.(figs.44 and 45) There were very few people around. We were usually the only guests sitting in their pretty garden at the edge of the water. The sun was not too hot. There was only one souvenir shop, and no advertisement hoarding at all. Yet I do remember that the locally bottled fizzy lemonade was labelled 'Spit!'.(figs.46 and 47)

44

45

46

47

Of course everything was Belgian or French, including the cuisine, which made a change from the habitual curries in Kenya. It was also a novelty to meet holidaymakers from

West Africa. The list of attractions was endless: the sandy beaches and clear water, no crocodiles or hippos, the abundant flora, the calm, the nearby mountain gorilla sanctuary, the mountains themselves, some of them active volcanos, the view of the lake at night with the orange glow of molten lava colouring the clouds above. Paradise!

One of the other hotel guests was a Belgian vulcanologist arrived from Uganda. At his suggestion, we somehow arranged to share a taxi with him back to Kampala, so giving us the pleasure of a stay en route in Uganda's Queen Elizabeth National Park on Lake Edward with its abundant wild-life. Euphoria seems to have drawn a veil over how we finally returned to Nakuru and whether we were refunded the unused flight tickets back to Nairobi.

# 7

# 'Kwa heri, Joe!'

Not many weeks after we had settled into our first married home back at Nakuru, Shell moved me, like a pawn on a chessboard, to a job in Nairobi. We were allotted the grand house with garden (and cat) of one of the senior managers, absent on long home leave.(fig.48) It was in the capital's most affluent neighbourhood, Muthaiga. The privilege of living there was soon spoilt by a growing sickly smell in the house. When it became too much to bear, I called in Shell's property maintenance people. They unlocked the cellar in which the manager had put away his valuables. Among them he had left hanging to ripen, and presumably forgotten, an entire cluster of bananas. Now a rotten, dripping column, it was alive with ants and other insects.

48

The time for my own home leave was approaching. It seemed the company was satisfied with my performance since they indicated that they would ask London to send me out for a second contract.

We returned to England in July 1959 and immediately set off for Austria in time for the Salzburg Festival. With the help of the local Shell office, we managed two operas. The one leaving the strongest impression was Gluck's *Orfeo* in the arcaded *Felsenreitschule*[23] under the baton of Herbert von Karajan. Curiously, the Shell manager in Salzburg reported that his Vienna head office had been in touch about me.

On our return from Austria to our notified base in England, my parents' house in the New Forest, they told me that Shell's London office had been asking urgently for my

---

[23] Cliff Riding School

whereabouts. It turned out that the company needed somebody to be PA to the Managing Director of Shell Austria in Vienna. The background to this was that the State Treaty giving Austria its independence had been signed by the occupying powers (which included the USSR) in 1955, but negotiations were still ongoing about the compensation owed by the Austrian government to Shell and Mobil for assets seized by the Nazis, then 'liberated' by the Red Army. After the war they had been taken over by Austria's State Oil Corporation. Perhaps it was thought my knowledge of Russian and German could be useful.

Nothing more was heard and we continued enjoying our leave, but as the autumn advanced we were beginning to think of getting back to the African sunshine. In December, when we had run through most of our resources and were ready to get back to the sun, we suddenly heard that it was to be Vienna.

We arrived there in January, shivering in our light-weight clothes. I began to harbour second thoughts about 'Joe Shell', as the firm used to be called by disgruntled employees, akin to the notion of Orwell's 'Big Brother'. There had also been the shock when, after our hurried arrival in Vienna, it was only then revealed that my contract with Shell Austria carried a considerably reduced salary package.

My office looked across the Schubertring towards the Schwarzenbergplatz where stands the Soviet War Memorial, a semi-circular colonnade with, at its centre, a more than life-size figure in stone. According to the local joke this was the only Red Army soldier who did not shout 'Часы давай!'[24] He

---

[24] 'Hand over your watch!'

was the nearest I came to dealing with any Russians in Vienna. I had no idea at the time that I would before long spend ten years teaching languages at Marlborough College, followed by twenty years in a rewarding official job in Britain's relations with Russia.[25]

After no more than a year in the Austrian capital, during which our first child was born, it was suddenly decided that the 'pawn' was to go back to Africa, to Cameroon to be their sales representative in Yaoundé, the capital. Only on enquiry did I learn that the real business centre in Cameroon, like Shell's primary office, was in the port city of Douala. Anyway, I was reluctant to take my wife and infant daughter to live in a colony where there was active insurgency, fed by arms from Eastern Europe. Even today Cameroon is referred to as a high-risk country to visit.

So I said, '*Kwa heri,* Joe!' At the age of twenty-eight, the pawn-worm had turned. We left Shell and took back control, encouraged in our new dawn by the simple lesson from Loitokitok, namely that daunting challenges sometimes have to be faced, but they can be surmounted. Indeed, such a lesson applied in very large measure to the four emerging countries which so long ago enriched my life.

---

[25] See my memoir *Speak Clearly into the Chandelier: Cultural Politics between Britain and Russia 1973–2000* with foreword *by John Le Carré.* (Curzon; 2000)

# Afterword

Without the skills and kindly care of the Stanhope Mews West medical practice and of the doctors and staff at the Chelsea and Westminster Hospital, the Royal Brompton and, latterly, the Royal Marsden, I would not have survived into my ninetieth year to write this little book and to see it through to realisation. No less important were the kind thoughts of parishioners at St. Paul's Knightsbridge and of the vicar, The Revd. Canon Alan Gyle.

For their active support, I am indebted to my family, not least to my granddaughter and fellow wordsmith, Georgina Roberts, at The Times. Charlie, her lawyer brother, supplied my cover portrait holding the Makonde snake stick. The rest of the photographs are mine, unless otherwise acknowledged. My cousin, Jonathan Roberts MSc, CEng, MICE, kindly produced the especially amended maps, aided by the fact that some thirty years after me he had come to know, through work like myself, many of the places mentioned. Emma Tristram, another family member and retired editor, gave me invaluable advice.

I am particularly grateful to Karen Jenkins who generously gave her time and expertise with matters outside my IT comfort zone.

I must also acknowledge the friendly encouragement and, in several cases, the practical help of Brigitte Chatenet, Simon Cobley, Martin Dewhirst, Pamela Griffiths, Simon Holdcroft, Brook Horowitz, Jag of Snappysnaps Chelsea, Lisa Maybus, Pam Mullin and Joanna Ward. I am particularly grateful to my dear friend, Ann Morrison, for the quiet writing time at her cottage in Kent. She is partially sighted, and it was important to have the benefit of her comments while listening to drafts read aloud.

Finally, I wish to thank the Outward Bound Trust. Fortified by my experience of their movement, I strive to overcome self-doubt and fear. Producing this book was my way of rising, with the help of my publisher, to the challenge of learning that I had an incurable illness.

John C Q Roberts
Chelsea, September 2022